AF326767

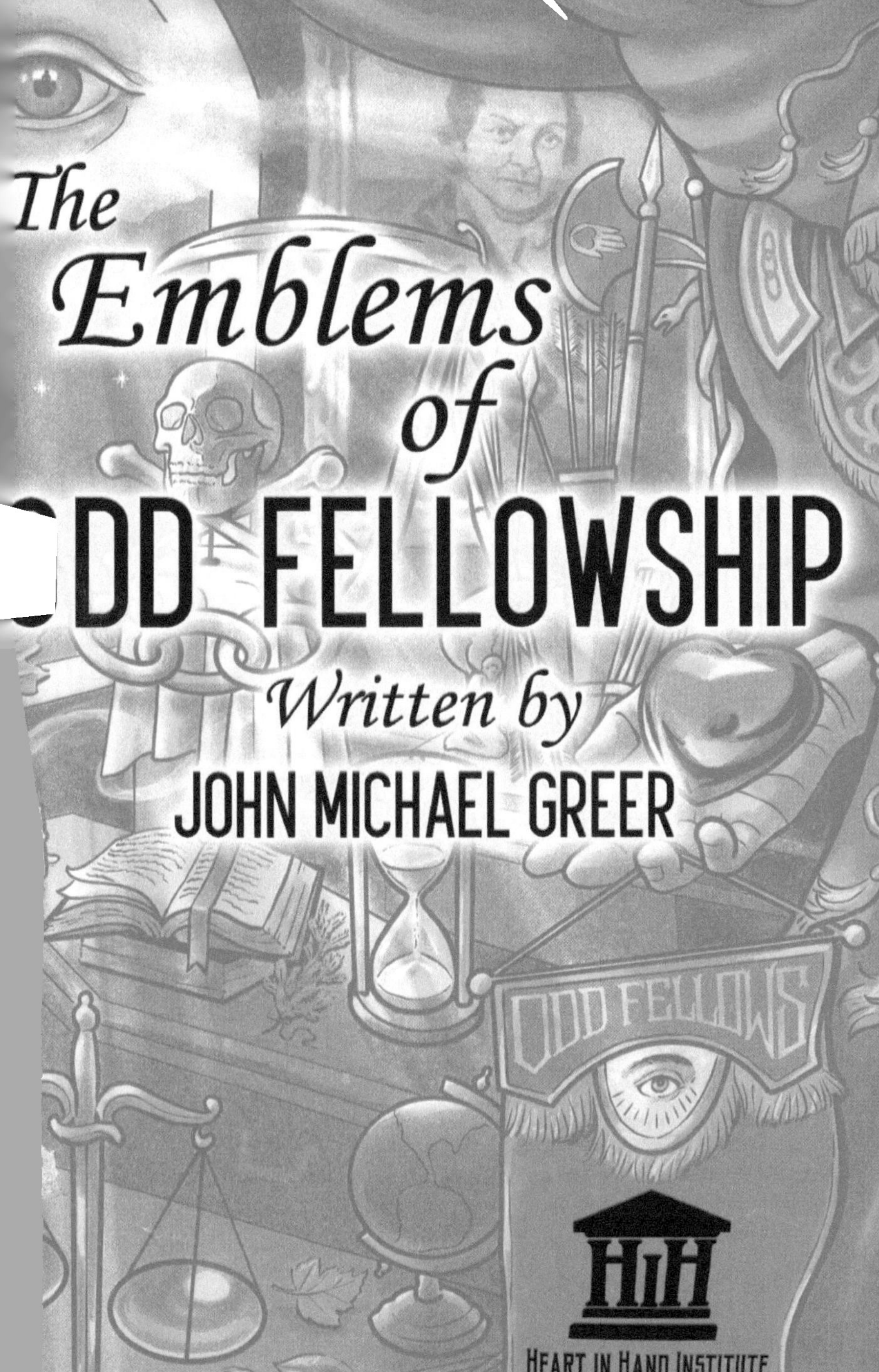
The
Emblems
of
ODD FELLOWSHIP
Written by
JOHN MICHAEL GREER
ODD FELLOWS
HiH
HEART IN HAND INSTITUTE

"Truth in the abstract – pure truth, freed from the attributes of materiality – cannot as easily be received and understood by man in the flesh, as when presented in a material garb. Hence parables and apologues, which are but word-emblems, are so acceptable among all nations; and this, too, is why, in all ages, the various objects in nature have been used as symbols. Humanity seems to require such representations. They are found in use as far as history reaches among the mists of the past. Their language seems the only one that escaped and survives the confusion of Babel."

- A. B. Grosh, "The Manual of Odd Fellowship"

Contents

Foreword

S ymbols have been a means of human communication since the very beginning of civilization. Tally marks first emerged in ancient Sumer as a means of keeping records free of the volatility of human memory. Many Asian writing systems evolved from pictograms representing everyday items of life. Even the Latin alphabet with which this text is written evolved over thousands of years from symbols in ancient Greece, Phoenicia, and Etruria; for example, the capital letter "A" is the inverted head of an ox.

Odd Fellowship, in its current form, coalesced in the early 19th Century as a means of mutual aid for the working masses. At the time, those masses were largely illiterate and incapable of reading extensively. Our founders wisely chose a means of communication which would be effective in reaching the literate and illiterate alike. Religious traditions of Europe had long used symbols for the same purpose, as in the example of Saint Patrick teaching the Holy Trinity through the use of Ireland's native shamrock. Members of that era would have been very familiar with the use of symbols to teach religious concepts from their experiences during worship services. Adopting that same method of communication for the principles of Odd Fellowship was a natural choice for our founders.

Thus, Odd Fellowship draws on a rich cultural history of symbology for communication and has amassed a large collection of symbols for teaching important concepts. Two hundred years ago, the meanings of those symbols would have been very common knowledge among members but, with the advancement of time, much of that meaning and context has been lost to modern readers. Noted scholar and author John Michael Greer has built a critical bridge to the past, bringing that knowledge into the present where we may all benefit from it, with this book. His research has made each of the symbols herein easily understandable to the modern Odd Fellow.

Over the course of its history, as Odd Fellowship has grown and changed, its symbols have followed suit. Where there were once five Degrees of Odd Fellowship beyond the Initiatory Degree, now there are only three. This book sheds light on the original meanings of our symbols and what they taught and indicates ways in which they have changed, grown, expanded, or been discarded – like so many other aspects of Odd Fellowship. It gives a thorough and complete look at the various symbols of Odd Fellowship, allowing the modern reader to appreciate what our forbearers would have learned from them and what we, ourselves, can learn from them today.

– Toby Hanson, PGM, PGP

Introduction

The traditions of the Odd Fellows Lodge and Encampment include a series of emblems – symbolic pictures that are used to teach many of the essential concepts of Odd Fellowship. At the present time, these emblems tend to receive little attention in lodge and even less out of it. They have a role in the degree ceremonies of the Order, and appear on the borders of lodge and encampment charters, but few Odd Fellows have any clear idea of their meaning and importance.

One of the main causes of this neglect, and one of the barriers that lies in the way of understanding these emblems and their meanings, is a historical shift in the way we use and think about symbols. In earlier times, people learned to read symbols as an ordinary part of growing up and getting an education. Nowadays, most of us have never developed this skill; compared to our ancestors, in fact, we might well be called symbolically illiterate.

In nineteenth-century literature, writers could make the briefest reference to a story from the Bible, an incident from Greek mythology, or some other common source of metaphors, and be confident that readers would catch the reference, read its meanings and understand the message it was supposed to convey. Thus early steam locomotives were often called "iron Jehus" because their speed, which reached the unheard-of rate of thirty miles an hour, reminded people

at once of the furious chariot toward a better and more con-
structive approach to living in the world.

The material in this booklet is intended, then, as an ABC
for the beginning reader of Odd Fellowship's symbols. I have
not tried to cover the whole realm of Odd Fellow symbolism
(a topic for a much larger book), but simply to show how the
twenty-two emblems of the Odd Fellows Lodge and Encampment can be understood as a guide to our Order's principles
and ideals. Those who are interested in learning more about
the language of the Order's symbolism will find plenty of
food for thought in the elements of Lodge and Encampment
symbolism. I have not covered, and in the work of the other
units of the Order, all of which have a rich symbolism of their
own.

My role in this work has been almost entirely that of a
compiler and editor. The text is based on discussions of the
Odd Fellow emblems drawn from old manuals and histories
of Odd Fellowship, many of them quite rare nowadays, where
the symbolic meaning of the emblems is discussed at length.
The passages discussing the degrees are taken from Paschal
Donaldson's "Odd Fellows' Pocket Companion," written in
1875; the discussions of each of the emblems have been com-
piled from a variety of works, which are listed at the end of
this booklet.

It seemed unnecessary to add anything to the material from
the sources, which illuminate the ideals of Odd Fellowship
through the emblems of the Order in a clear and meaningful
way. I hope that other Odd Fellows will find these emblems
and their lessons as enjoyable, and as thought-provoking, as I
have.

– John Michael Greer, PGP

Emblems of the Initiatory Degree

It may well be considered an important period in a man's life when he passes the threshold of Odd Fellowship. The duties taught him, and the lessons inculcated throughout the progress he may make in the Order will tend, if he be true to his nature, to his moral and intellectual advancement, and consequently to his happiness. He should therefore prepare his mind for the task he has undertaken, and determine to be attentive to the instructions he is about to receive.

Man gropes his way through life in darkness and in doubt. His reason and his moral nature are dark, and by his own passions he brings himself into a state of slavery more bitter than any human bondage. If he suffer himself to be led away captive by them, he must at last be dragged to the lowest depths of wretchedness. He should, therefore, seek to liberate himself from their grasp, until by virtuous perseverance he acquires a knowledge of himself, his duty and his destiny. Then the light breaks in upon him, and he sees clearly the path he must tread.

The lessons of the Initiatory Degree are Fraternity and Secrecy, and its regalia is a plain white collar. Its emblems are the All-Seeing Eye, the Three Links, the Skull and Crossbones, and the Scythe.

The All-Seeing Eye

Emblem of Omniscience

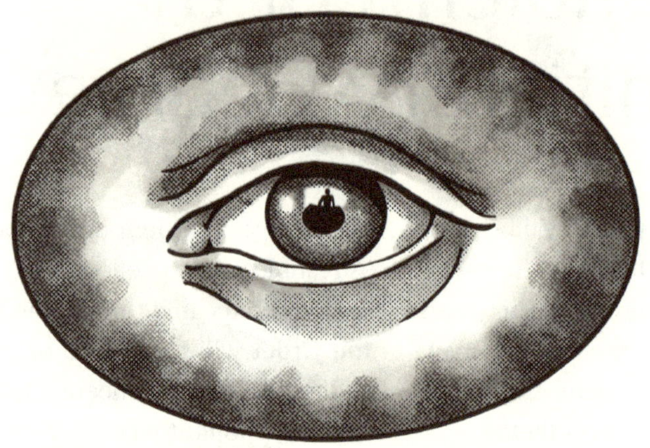

The eye enveloped in a blaze of light and glory reminds us that the omniscience of God pierces into every secret of the heart. All our thoughts and actions are to Him revealed, as soon as the one is conceived or the other done. Let us therefore so regulate our conduct that we may not fear the scrutinizing eye of anyone. Let us always do the right for its own sake more than for the hope of reward or the fear of reproof.

As Odd Fellows, let us always remember those expressive words that cannot be too deeply imprinted on our minds, "Thou, God, seest me!" For the eye of the Lord is in every place, beholding the evil and the good. We may also, in this connection, remind ourselves that "a wholesome tongue is a tree of life;" that the secrets we have promised to keep inviolate will never be divulged, except by a man devoid of the principles of honor. On entering or leaving the lodge room, we note the All-Seeing Eye as a reminder of the instruction at our initiation, and it serves to keep us steadfast in our integrity.

This emblem also presents us with the idea of secrecy. The fellowship into which we come on admission to the Odd Fellows is a secret fellowship, in that it has secrets which are only known by those who have been admitted among us. In Odd Fellowship there are pass- words and signs and grips, each of which have great importance to those who receive them. There are obligations solemn and binding, and they are secret, and in their secrecy is hidden their charms. Here are our impressive lessons, and the efficacy of our Order. Destroy them, and the fellowship, with all its appropriateness, is gone. Though the outside world is ignorant of the lessons we have received and the obligations we have taken, yet God is not ignorant.

The Three Links

Emblem of Friendship, Love and Truth

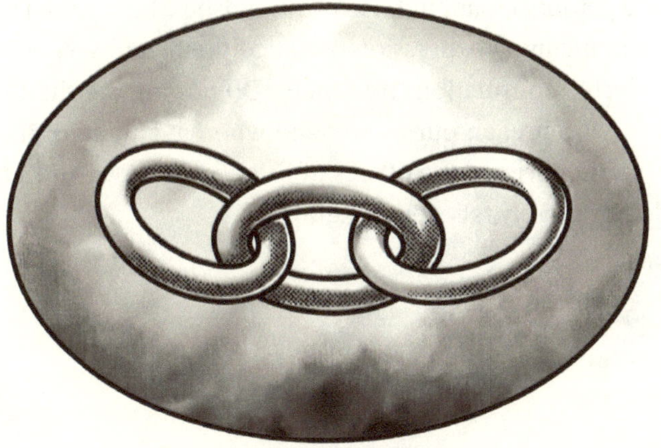

This emblem directs our attention to the three great principles of our Order, which together form the leading motto of Odd Fellowship. These three links form a chain which binds the members of our Order together in the closest union. It is a threefold cord that may not easily be broken. It is a union that makes the banded a strength and a power. They go forth into the world to accomplish in their united capacity what singly and alone they could not do.

The three links are emblematical of the chain by which we are bound together in Friendship, Love and Truth. We are anchored by them to the steadfast purposes of our covenant, and are cautioned to keep them untarnished and free from rust, as a chain is only as strong as its weakest link.

The three links represent the all-encircling chain of sympathy that unites us as one in our aims, labors, and rewards, and reminds us that we are thus bound for our own and each other's welfare. Friendship, love and truth extended toward man by his brother universally would make of this world a comparative paradise. It would turn aside half the ills that "flesh is heir to," and produce an amount of happiness that would astonish mankind itself. "Friendship, Love and Truth" is no unmeaning expression. Practice them, and you at least will derive consolation from them. Do not imitate the theorizers, who preach our motto, and who have none of its life and spirit; perform the offices of Friendship, Love and Truth – do not merely talk about them.

The Skull And Crossbones

Emblem of Mortality

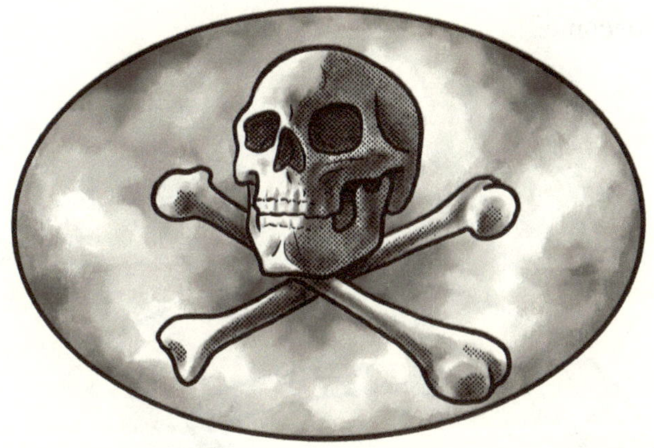

The skull and crossbones remind us of our mortality, and warn us to so conduct ourselves here on earth that heaven may be our reward in the hereafter. We are further taught to decently place in mother earth the mortal remains of our brethren and keep green in our memories an affectionate remembrance of them.

Who can look upon human bones, bleached by the bleak winds and rains of succeeding winters, or who can look on the pale dead, coffined for sepulchre, without hearing a voice speaking to the living, saying, "As I am now, so you shall be"? This emblem bids us get ready for the end of earthly existence; it urges us to be ready for the summons that sooner or later will be served upon us.

The decree of Heaven is, "Dust thou art, and unto dust thou shalt return." We all await the inevitable hour. What is our life? It is but a vapor, that appears for a little time and then vanishes away. Where are the myriads of the human family that have lived and figured on the earth? They all sleep with their ancestors, and the places that once knew them shall know them no more forever. Let us seriously meditate on these monitors of "what we are sure to be, and what we may soon become."

The Scythe

Emblem of Transience

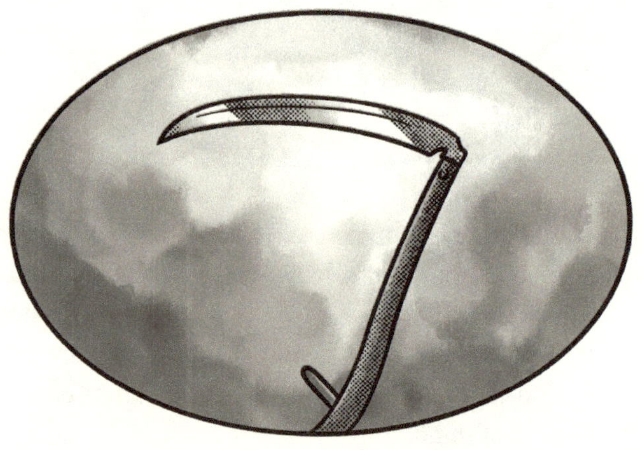

This emblem teaches us of the end of all earthly things – of the common lot of all mankind. It requires but a few months for the growth of the grass each season, and then the harvest comes. "All flesh is grass, and the glory of man as the flower of the grass; the grass withereth, and the flower thereof falleth away."

The scythe reminds us that as the grass falls before the mower's scythe, so we, too, fall before the touch of Time. We are as the flowers of the field, blooming and bright today, while tomorrow we fall withered and decayed into the bosom of our mother earth. Old Time, with his unerring scythe, is on our track – we cannot escape him. Let us engrave this truth on our hearts, that there is not a moment to waste: that in the brief time allotted to us on earth, the good or ill we accomplish is all of us that shall live among men.

Emblems of the First Degree

No man is entirely without the instinct of friendship. The natural affections never completely die; yet the kindly sensibilities often become blunted with time, and the heart, hardened by selfishness, forgets the tenderness with which it once regarded the sorrows of the distressed. Associations for purposes of benevolence serve to banish selfishness, and to keep alive and active the kindly sensibilities of the heart, by enforcing an observance of social and humane duties.

In an association for mutual relief, men of all classes and conditions enter into a covenant to help and support, to protect and defend, to advise and admonish each other. Covenants have existed in all nations and among all peoples. We find them in every walk of life. Many of these, however, are mere compacts of business; the covenant of brotherhood is one more holy and sublime; it is designed to remove the obstacles that interpose between the hearts of men.

The lesson of the First Degree is Friendship, and its regalia is a pink collar. Its emblems are the Bow and Arrows, the Quiver, and the Bundle of Sticks.

The Bow & Arrows

Emblem of War

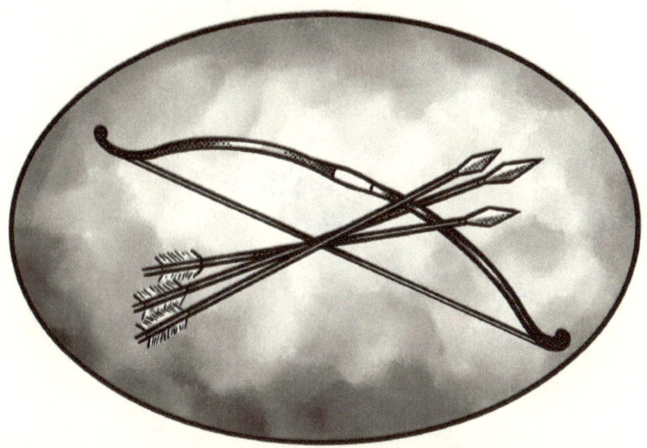

The bow and arrows remind us that "we war against vice in all its forms." Thus they teach us to guard the loved one from evil, to repel impending danger, and to secure safety. They are not to be used wantonly, or to destroy aught but evil and wrong – only for benefit and salvation to innocence and suffering. The unstrung bow also teaches the benefit of relaxation from undue tension of mind or body, when recreation can safely besought.

As the marksman prides himself on the certainty of his aim, in turn, so should we study to make our generous deeds sure. We must not perform our good offices at random, but so regulate and direct them as to render them serviceable at the proper time, and place, and circumstance.

The Quiver

Emblem of Preparation

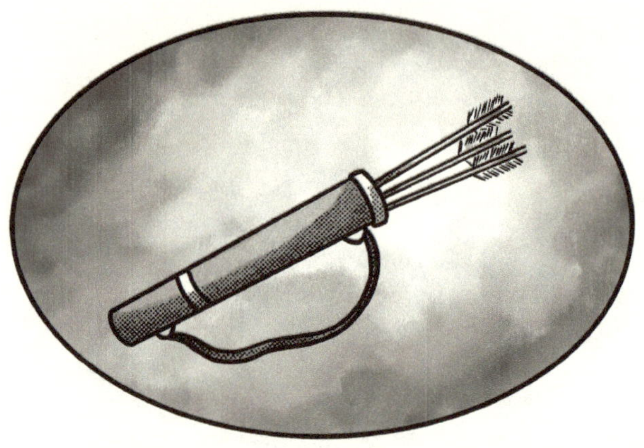

The quiver full of arrows reminds us of David and. Jonathan and the covenant made between them. The true Odd Fellow will always have his quiver and his bow ready to guard a brother from danger, or to promote his welfare. This emblem should teach us, as Odd Fellows, to be ready to make all laudable efforts to save a brother when he is in peril, and to watch over his interests when they are threatened. Just as the bow teaches the need for relaxation, the full quiver as impressively teaches the importance of preparation for action, even in our hours of ease and enjoyment.

The Bundle of Sticks

Emblem of Strength in Union

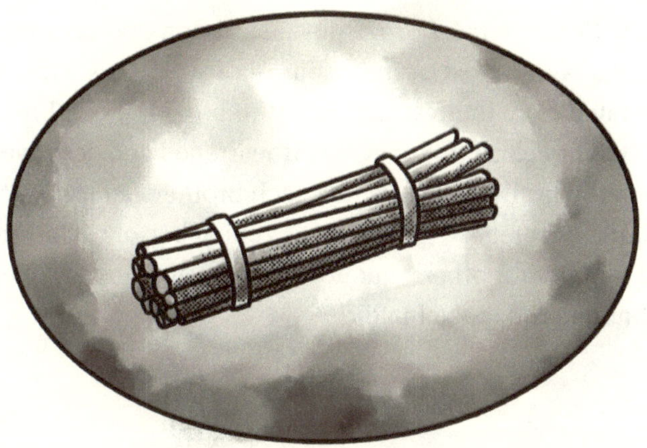

The bundle of sticks inculcates the importance of con-centrated effort, as expressed in the axiom, "in union there is strength." It reminds us of the power of each member to sustain and be sustained by the others, when all are bound into one bundle, making the interests and labors of all the common property of each.

While a man may be engaged in a good cause, and make laudable and efficient efforts for success in it, yet single-hand-ed and alone he can accomplish but little compared to what he could accomplish with good and efficient helpers. A man may have very benevolent designs, a large heart to do good, but alone he may be almost powerless to accomplish that good. There is ability, when banded together – united in heart and effort – to accomplish a great and important work for the good of others. A comparatively small obstacle may prevent a single individual from carrying a design of benevolence into effect, when a number of men associated together can easily perform it.

If we wish to obtain success commensurate with our efforts, we must pursue the end for which we strive unitedly, and with one mind and purpose. Disunion and uncertainty of aims is the most certain source of weakness. One rod, separated from the rest, can easily be broken – one brother, isolated by selfishness, may be disheartened and destroyed – but in the firmly bound bundle each brother can easily resist evil and accomplish good. Let us remember our obligations and wait not for others, but do what we can, though we each be but one rod in the bundle.

Emblems of the Second Degree

Brotherly love dwells among those who meet for the purpose of benevolence. The fraternal relation is one around which cluster the best feelings of our nature, and he who becomes duly impressed with a sense of the obligations of this relationship can be controlled neither by selfishness nor by indifference. The principles we profess are such as to refine the powers and faculties which constitute the dignity and glory of man – and the greatest of these is love.

Justice, temperance and charity are the duties of all men, and we should exercise all three in our dealings with our brethren and with the world. We should do with promptness and alacrity all the good in our power to our fellow-man. We should teach charity to others both by precept and by example. To cultivate a generous spirit of kindness, to wake up the sympathies and purge the heart of its selfishness, is the noblest mission in which man can engage.

The lesson of the Second Degree is Brotherly Love, and its regalia is a blue collar. Its emblems are the Axe, the Heart and Hand, the Globe, the Ark of the Covenant, and the Serpent.

The Axe

Emblem of Pioneering

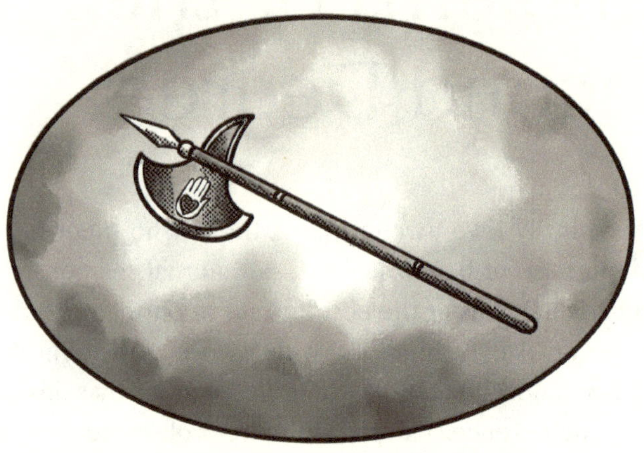

The axe is used by the hardy pioneer, who clears a way through the trackless forest with unwearied stroke and unfaltering arm. It reminds us that we are pioneers in the pathway of life, smoothing the rough places and removing all obstacles to the weak and the faltering. Equally, we must clear away the growth of prejudice and passion from within ourselves, in order to fully profit from the influences of fraternity in our lodge, our Order, and in the family of man.

In many lodges it was once customary to collect donations for the needy and distressed on the Warden's axe, which had painted on the side presented for the donation the expressive Heart and Hand.

The Heart and Hand

Emblem of Sincerity

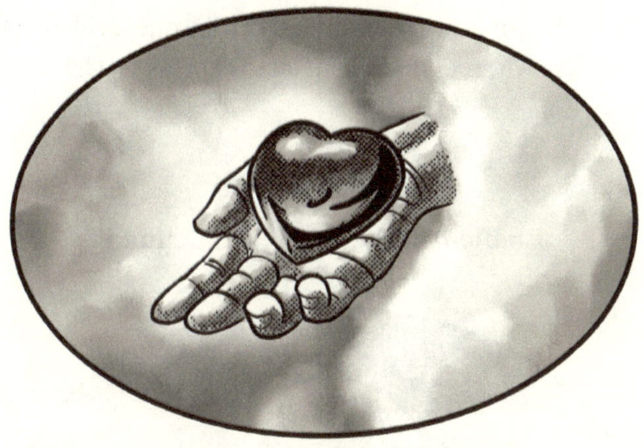

The heart and hand teach us that whatever the hand finds to do, the heart should go forth in unison. The work entrusted to us to perform should be one of love, pursued from the promptings of the heart and free from the taint of mercenary or selfish motives. There should be no concealment of feelings and purposes among brethren; our greetings should be of the heart as well as of the hand.

The command of our laws is that we visit the sick, relieve the distressed, bury the dead and educate the orphan. What our hands find to do in these respects, therefore, we should do cheerfully and with a whole heart, not grudgingly and unwillingly. True friendship goes out with alacrity to the service required of it. Heart and hand should go forth in concert in the cause of suffering. humanity; they must not be divided in their energies.

This emblem has a special reference to the help that one brother should give another in our Order, and the spirit with which he should bestow his assistance. It may also remind us that whether the hand is extended to a brother in the first link or in the grip of an advanced degree, the heart should always go with the hand in the greeting. As Odd Fellows let our hand-greeting be a friendly and cordial one, evidencing to those whom we greet that we mean to express real friendship.

The Globe

Emblem of the World of Mankind

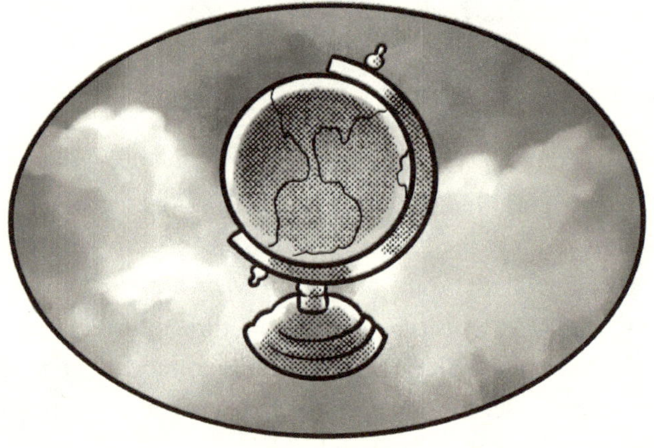

The globe reminds us that the field of our labors is a wide one and coextensive with the globe. There is much to learn and to teach in this great field, over which our brethren are so widely scattered. Until the tear of the sorrow-stricken has ceased to flow, and humanity is everywhere swayed in its actions by the divine lessons of peace and good will, our work must continue to occupy our time and thoughts.

The Ark of the Covenant

Emblem of the Divine Presence

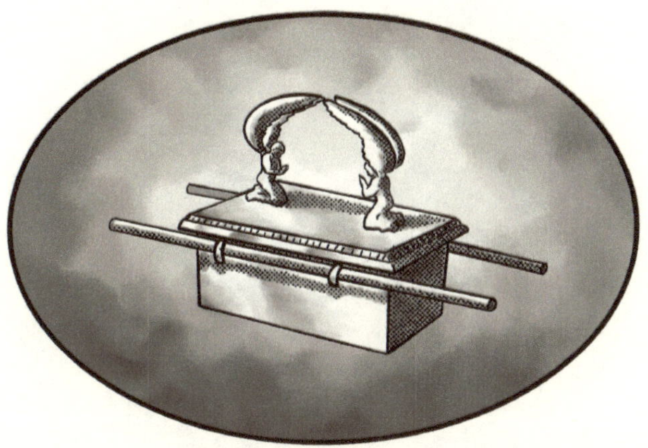

The Ark of the Covenant was placed within the Holy of Holies: that is, within the second veil of the Tabernacle, and in the innermost part of the Temple. It is therefore a most solemn emblem, suggestive of all things most sacred.

The Ark was the receptacle of the two tables of stone containing the Ten Commandments, which describes man's duties to his God as well as to his neighbor and fellow man. It also contained the manna by which the children of Israel were fed in the wilderness, and the rod of Aaron that budded forth. As the preservation of the Ark was an unceasing object of care to the Israelites, we are reminded by this emblem to be solicitous for the preservation of our Order's laws, and to ever hold them in such remembrance and respect, that our conduct in the world may bring no reproach upon our brotherhood.

The Serpent

Emblem of Wisdom

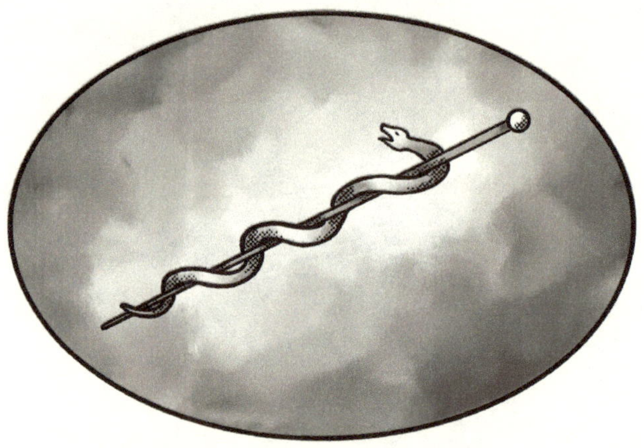

The serpent teaches us that without wisdom to guide and control our actions, we are as a ship without a rudder, at the mercy of the warring winds and angry waves. It also reminds us of the brazen serpent erected by Moses to heal the stricken Israelites. Let us, then, seek wisdom that our work may be done to the best advantage.

While we should be harmless as doves, let us also be wise as serpents. We must suffer no man – brother though he profess to be - to deceive us by false tokens. All are not Odd Fellows who take the name. All are not our co-laborers who claim to be so. He who is selfish, or avaricious, or uncharitable, is not our brother. We should reform him, if we can, but we must not reveal to him our secrets. Let us do our own work, and not make him a partner in it.

Emblems of the Third Degree

Truth is that grand virtue which deals plainly and honestly in all actions, without disguise, without falsehood, and without hypocrisy; it comprehends all that is wise and good; it is the vital spirit of every community which is well founded among men. Truth presents us with a rule to ascertain what virtue is, and guides us into its personal possession. Truth is essentially the only foundation of confidence, and confidence is the only bond of association among the wise, the good, and the intelligent. To it we are indebted for the whole sum of happiness enjoyed in time.

The man who does good, and speaks truth, reminds us that we are made in the image of God, whose essential properties are goodness and truth. Though truth is an attribute of Deity, it has been made attainable by man, that his race might be blessed and improved. Let us, then, be true to our professions. Let our walk and conversation in life be such that the world will be compelled to acknowledge the sublime theory we teach.

The lesson of the Third Degree is Truth, and its regalia is a scarlet collar. Its emblems are the scales and sword, the Bible, the hourglass, and the coffin.

The Scales and Sword

Emblems of Justice

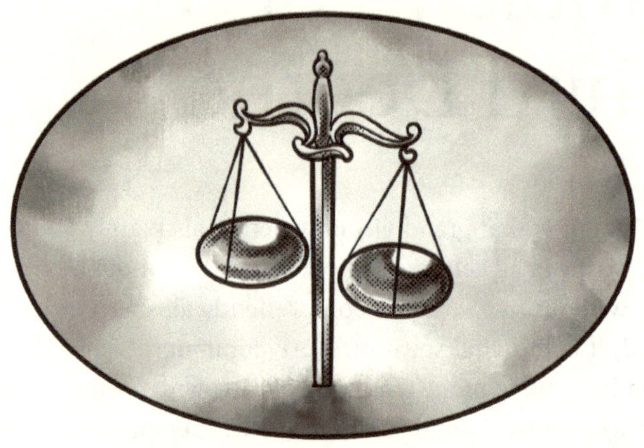

The scales and sword remind us that justice and mercy should be administered without reference to social differences. Whatever distinctions there may be in society outside of the fraternity of Odd Fellows, there are no distinctions within it. The rich and the poor, the high and the low, the learned and the unlearned, meet on a common level, and as brothers unite for the promotion of benevolence and truth.

The scales represent the weighing of evidence and opinions, to determine their true values and relations; and remind us that though the love of family and country are natural, and may be made useful, yet we must not stop with these, nor array them in conflict with our more comprehensive duties to mankind and to God. The sword represents the defending and enforcing power of righteousness, and reminds us that God requires us to decide justly, after weighing equitably, and to defend the right even unto death if need be.

Let us weigh well our conduct, and do unto others according to the injunctions of the Golden Rule. Let us consider that the sword of punishment, like that of Damocles, is suspended over our own heads. Temper justice with mercy, but act for the general good.

The Bible

Emblem of Spiritual Truth

The Bible is a lamp to our feet and a light to our path; it is placed among our emblems because it is the fountain whence we draw instruction, the storehouse whence our precepts are derived, and most of our emblems are found in its pages. What you have been told of the sacred contents of the Ark of the Covenant might be appropriately be repeated here. It contains directions and counsel for every phase, circumstance, and condition of life.

The Hourglass

Emblem of Time

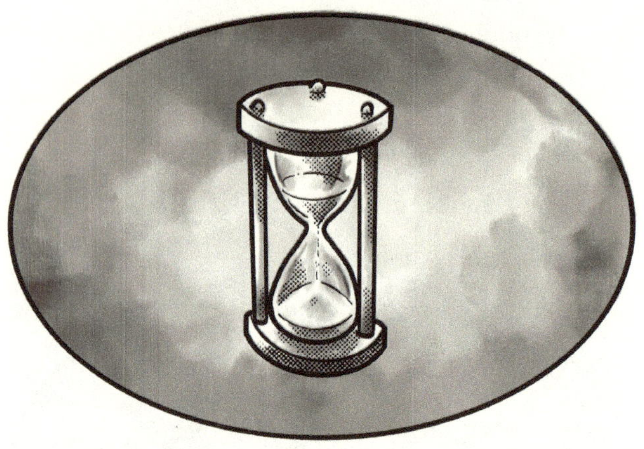

The hourglass is symbolic of the flight of time. We should therefore improve each passing hour, so that we may enter the great hereafter with life's labor well done. We are reminded that "procrastination is the thief of time," and that constant and persistent labors are bound to result in deserved and merited success. As the sands of the hourglass incessantly run down, so every breath we take but shortens life and brings its end nearer. "Time and tide wait for no man." We should do with our might what our hands find to do, for time passed never can be recovered.

The world, at its brightest and best, is of time, subject to all Time's chances and changes, and this emblem reminds us that all the goodliness and fashion thereof is but as "the grass that withereth and the flower that fadeth." The hourglass ad-monishes us to improve the moments as they fly, in a manner that shall redound to the glory of God and our own and our neighbor's good. It also brings before us the great contrast between Time and Eternity.

The Coffin

Emblem of Completion

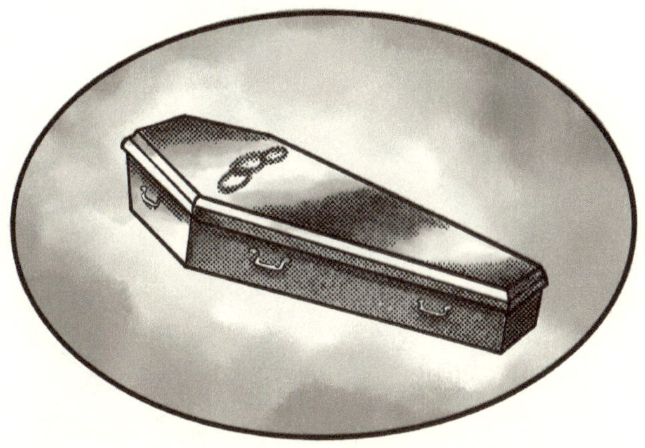

The coffin reminds us of the inevitable hour when dust shall return to dust and the mortal shall put on immortality. It behooves us so to regulate our lives and conduct here that we may depart hence with a well-founded hope and assurance of eternal happiness. As we know what we are and soon will be, let us make certain that our life's labors are well done, and that our labors deserve and receive heaven's choicest blessings.

The coffined one, cold in death, has passed through all the changes in life and come to its last great and important change. We shall each surely go down to the grave, and shall be numbered with the shrouded millions, while our character and influence, still left upon the stage of man, will be telling for the good ill of succeeding generations. If we have done good, the living will bless us in their memories, and if we have done evil, they will reproach and mourn our destructive influence.

Emblems of the Encampment Degrees

I n the Encampment, the emblems are not divided up among the degrees (as they are in the Odd Fellows Lodge), but are the common property of all three of the degrees of Patriarchal Odd Fellowship.

<u>The Patriarchal Degree</u>

The patriarchs of old, who dwelt in tents, whose employment was that of shepherds, and who passed their lives in the inculcation of the social virtues, were a happy because they were a good people. Imitate their pure example, and you will find the enjoyment which they so richly enjoyed.

Let the character and conduct of the Patriarchs of old be your study, and in all their good deeds, be you their imitator. Amid the corruptions of the world that beset them on every hand, they were ever true and faithful. They were devoted to all that was worthy of frail man's consideration. They lived not alone for themselves, but for their age and for all future time. Thus you should live. The possession of virtue such as theirs is far preferable to all the power and glory that this world might bestow.

Hospitality to the stranger, in particular, is a duty enjoined by God, who teaches us that, as He is the Father of all men, we are not to pause to inquire our brother's faith, or creed, or nation, before we render him the sympathy and aid he may need. He who succors the distressed, who gives food and rest to the hungry and weary, who comforts the broken-hearted, and raises the fallen, shall enjoy a pleasure far more desirable than wealth, or power, or fame.

The lessons of the Patriarchal Degree are Faith and Hospitality, and its regalia is a black collar.

The Golden Rule Degree

Human prejudice and intolerance are and have ever been the causes of more misery in the world than all other evils combined. Be it our duty to destroy their power, by asserting and maintaining the high birthright of humanity – by regarding and treating our brother as our equal, the child of our own benevolent Father, created in like form, and bearing the same image as ourselves. The evils that afflict our brother should be regarded as in a measure our own. If we injure him, we shall also injure ourselves. Whatever directly affects a member of the body, must remotely affect the entire structure. Man's misfortunes are our misfortunes, and his sufferings are ours.

As no two faces among the billions of the race of man now on earth are alike, so perhaps no two in this vast multitude of minds think alike. Difference of opinion, on religious subjects especially, has always existed. Should we despise our brother for this difference? Nay! He has the same right as ourselves to the enjoyment of his personal opinion, and may maintain it in opposition to the opinions of the whole world.

When the golden rule shall have exerted its power, and obtained its dominion over the world, men of all creeds and nations shall sit together, and the light of knowledge and of joy shall shine around and about them. Let us exert our utmost endeavors to hasten this most desirable period.

The lessons of the GoldenRule Degree are Hope and Tolerance, and its regalia is a black collar edged with gold.

The Royal Purple Degree

We live in a world of change, of sorrow and of pain; but we must struggle on, though beset with danger, toil and strife, through the wilderness of this world, to our destiny. Let us be stout of heart, and determine, through faith and energy, to overcome the obstacles that lie in our path. Let neither fear nor discouragement cause us to turn back, after we shall have once entered on our journey.

Let us take honesty for our guide along the way. However rough or uncouth he may seem, or whatever abuse may be heaped upon him by those who love him not, he will assuredly bring us at last to a peaceful and pleasant abode.

The road on which you are traveling may be a rough one. Difficulties may crowd around you to impede your progress. The path may be filled with obstacles that would intimidate a weak spirit; at times, it may be a cheerless and dreary way. Keep up the spirit; if your heart be strong and your faith hold fast, you will make your way to the goal you seek.

The lessons of the Royal Purple Degree are Charity and Perseverance, and its regalia is a purple collar edged with gold.

The emblems of the Encampment degrees are the three pillars, the Patriarch's tent, the pilgrim's scrip, sandals and staff, the altar of sacrifice, the tables of stone, cross and crescent, and the altar of incense.

The Three Pillars

Emblem of Faith, Hope and Charity

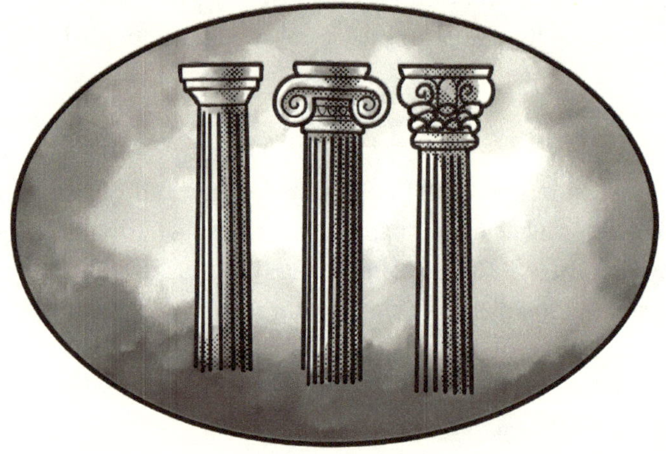

The three pillars are faith, hope and charity. With faith as our companion we steadfastly pursue our tasks, confident that our labors will eventually be rewarded.

Hope is the handmaid of faith; it cheers the sinking soul. in its hour of deep distress; it borders every cloud with a silver lining, and at last, conducts with serenity to the portals of death. Charity is the last yet the greatest of all, the brightest and best of the virtues. Let us always have faith in God, hope of immortality and charity to all mankind.

Every time we enter an Encampment, the three pillars remind us of the wisdom of humility, the strength of trust, and the beauty of kindness which brought us to the emblematic tent, and before its solemn altar. They also teach us to cherish and cultivate these treasures and virtues of the soul, by an observance of the great law of duty to God, to our neighbor and to ourselves.

The Patriarch's Tent

Emblem of Hospitality

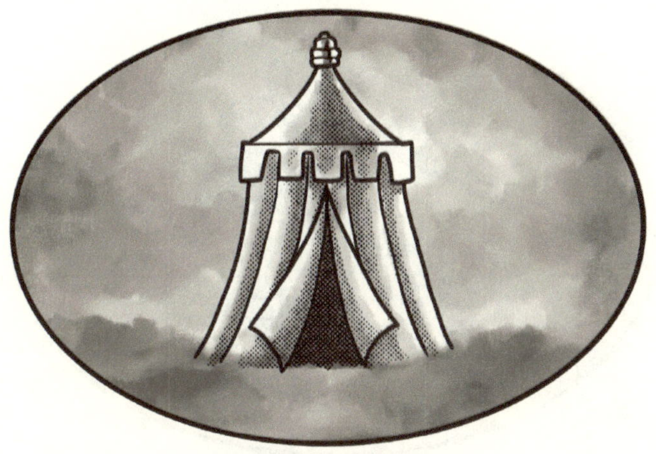

The Patriarch's tent is symbolic of peace, comfort and hospitality, the prominent characteristics of the shepherds of old. It is always represented open, to remind us that when we needed hospitality we found it, and should therefore be ready to grant it when needed by others. We may learn from this emblem to be true in all our expressed feelings, and be always ready to befriend and supply the wants of a wayworn and distressed traveler. "Be not forgetful to entertain strangers, for thereby some have entertained angels unawares."

The Patriarch's tent also reminds us of the pilgrimage of the Israelites from Egypt to the Promised Land. It is emblematic of our own journey through life, and we should profit by the many valuable lessons inculcated in this story. This emblem may remind us again of the slender hold we have on earth. "Here we have no continuing city, but we seek one to come."

The Pilgrim's Scrip, Sandals and Staff

Emblems of Pilgrimage

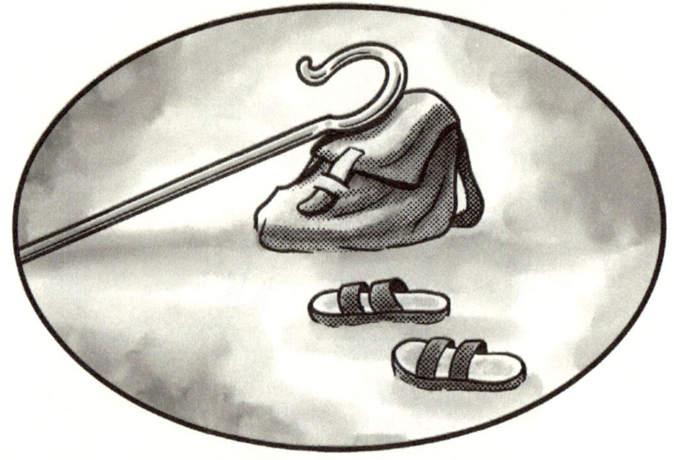

This emblem presents man as a traveler; being engaged in making an important journey he has prepared himself with scrip, sandals and staff. By these emblems we are reminded that life is a journey, and that our stay here is one of short duration.

We are further taught that we should not pursue our way without due preparation for the exigencies of the occasion. We are in duty bound to employ every instrumentality necessary and likely to facilitate our work and progress. We must remember that our duty is not fulfilled unless we do the best we can. The scrip, the sandals and the staff speak to us of preparations for a journey, not of a day, but of a lifetime – not measured by miles, but by years – not from place to place, but from the cradle to the coffin.

The Altar of Sacrifice

Emblem of Sacrifice

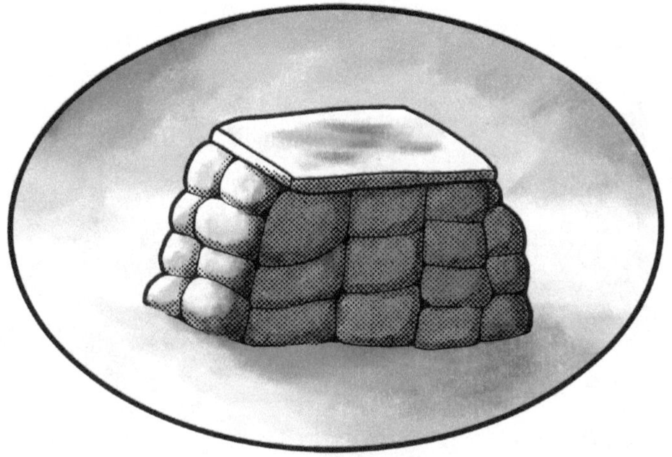

The altar of sacrifice reminds us that our selfish purposes and ungenerous impulses must be restrained and sacrificed on the altar of Friendship, Love and Truth; and it declares that no duty nor deed of well-doing should be neglected or evaded to indulge in any personal gratification or individual interest.

Weak and erring mortals that we are, we need the divine blessing and assistance on our every enterprise. Let our hearts be clean and contrite, and our labors a willing sacrifice for the redemption of humanity.

The Tables of Stone, Cross, and Crescent

Emblem of Toleration

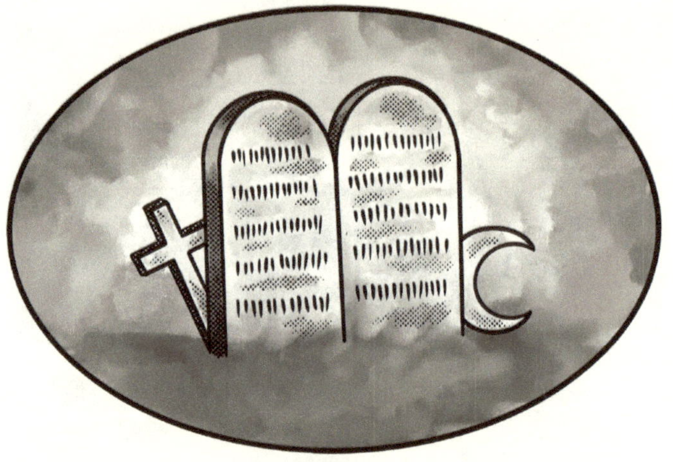

The two tables of stone remind us of the moral law by and under which we are bound to regulate all our thoughts and actions, and taught not to neglect our duty to God and our fellow man. The cross and crescent teach us toleration. The prejudices that grow up and are fostered by the pressure of education should be trampled underfoot, and every man enjoy the sacred right of worshipping God according to his own conscience.

As thought is free, our law eschews all bigotry, and leaves every man at full liberty to worship God according to the dictates of his conscience. Let us always practice unity in good works, wherein all agree, and toleration in opinions, wherein we differ.

The Altar of Incense

Emblem of Thanksgiving

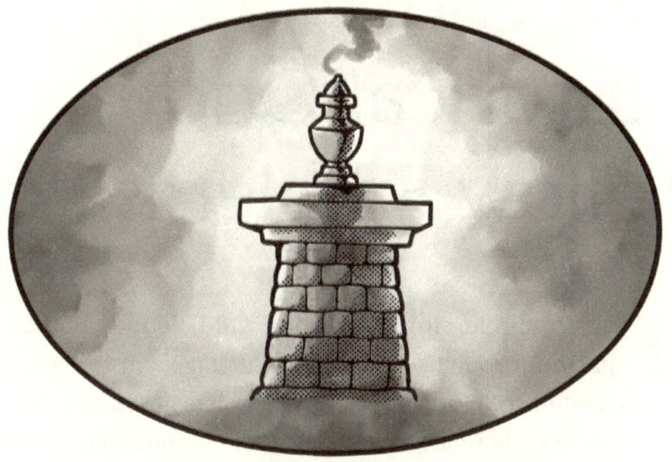

The altar of incense reminds us that we owe to the Almighty praise and thanksgiving for the many blessings we enjoy. We receive so much and return so little, that it should be a labor of love to express our gratitude. So, in our intercourse with our brethren, we should at all times return our thanks whenever due, and show our appreciation of any and every act of kindness. To know that our brotherly acts are appreciated makes the duty of doing good a positive pleasure.

May the heart of every Odd Fellow ever contain the pure incense of a true devotion to God and mankind, and may that incense be ever burning day and night like the incense on the holy altar in the Temple.

Appendix: Historical Odd Fellow Emblems

The symbolic alphabet of the Odd Fellow emblems passed through several different stages on the way to its present form. While most of the emblems have stayed the same since early times, or passed through minor alterations, some emblems that once had a part in the Order's ritual work were set aside in favor of others better suited to the evolving needs of Odd Fellowship. Three of the older emblems were transferred to the Rebekah Degree, where they now play an important role; several others have taken on other roles within the symbolic language of Odd Fellowship; the rest have simply lapsed into disuse.

These former emblems of the Order were the Sun, the Moon and Stars, the Lamb, the Bundle of Rods, the Rainbow, Moses' Rod, Noah's Ark, the Horn of Plenty, the Dove, Aaron's Rod, the Beehive, and the Shepherd's Crook. The Globe, now a symbol of the Second Degree, was originally two symbols - the Globe in Clouds and the Globe in Sun - and these can also be considered historical emblems, as much of their original meaning has been lost in the process of simplification.

Each of these historical emblems has been listed on the pages that follow, together with commentaries on the meaning of each emblem, drawn from old Odd Fellow handbooks.

The Sun

Emblem of Light

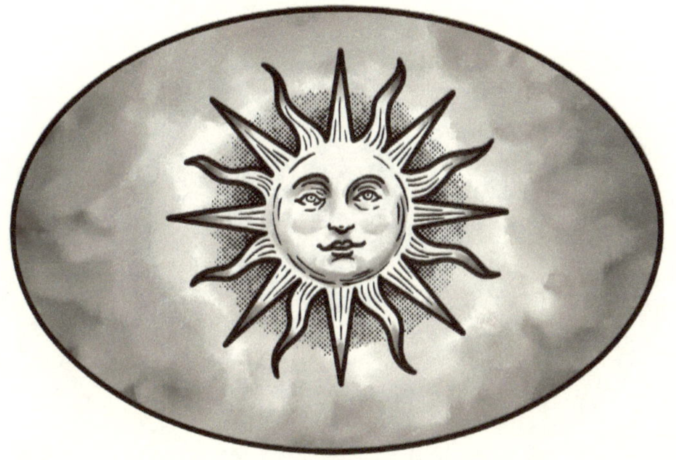

The sun is the emblem of power and vigor; the moon and stars are not only subordinate to it, but dependent on it. Truth is our great light. If we, in the course of our pilgrimage here on earth, realize its power in our hearts, permit it to control our actions, and in our turn reflect its strength upon others' hearts, we shall be the noblest benefactors of humanity.

The Moon and Stars

Emblem of Order

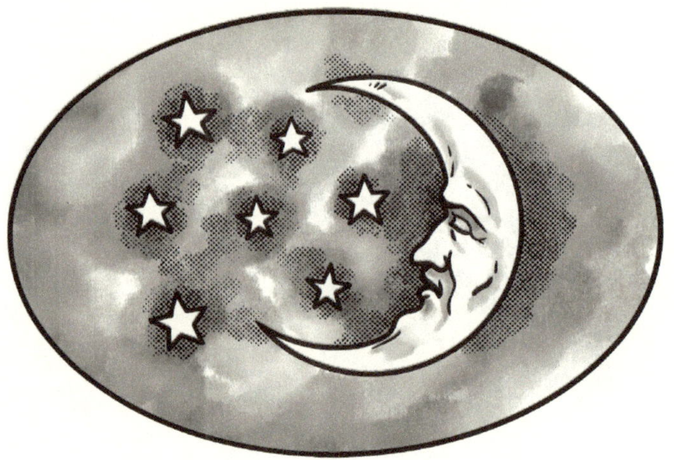

The moon and stars represent the exact and unerring laws of Nature, and teach us the necessity of system, order and regularity in the performance of all our duties, both in the lodge room and outside it. The moon, reflecting the light of the sun, also represents to us the welcome smiles of Friendship, Love and Truth, shining in the night of misfortune; and teaches us that as her rays are only reflected from a greater luminary, so all the glory and beauty of this earth, all the wisdom and goodness man can exhibit, are but reflections caught from the great Source of life, light and love.

The Lamb

Emblem of Innocence

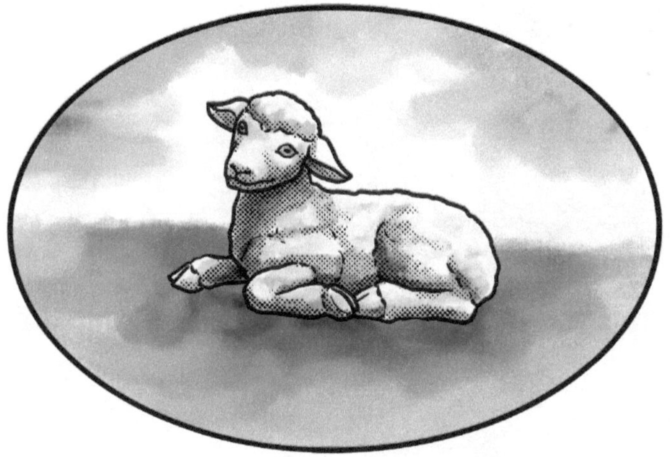

Innocence is one of the loveliest qualities which adorn human nature. The corrupt laugh at, and affect to despise it; but in their hearts they honor it. The temperate, the chaste, the benevolent, and the charitable, are beloved by all of humanity. Innocence of wrong-doing commends itself to all, and he who evinces it in his life and conduct may command the confidence of the whole world.

The Rainbow

Emblem of Safety

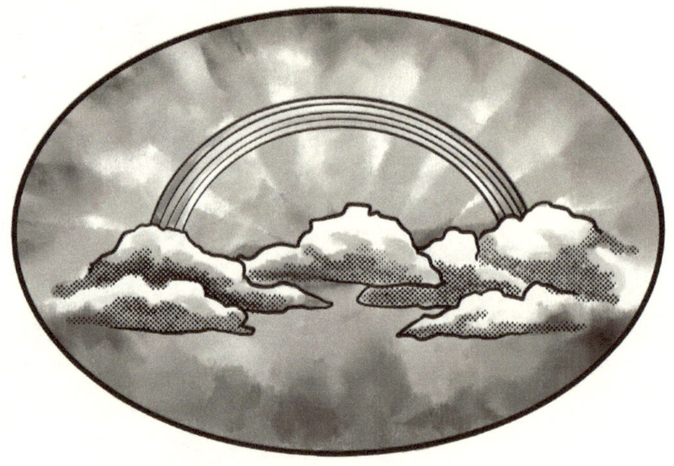

This is one of the most beautiful of nature's emblems, and of the most impressive in our Order. It reminds us of God's covenant with Noah for the safety of the world and mankind, and of our covenant with our brethren. When it appears in the heavens, "all woven with light," the true Odd Fellow will read its divine language with admiration, and its special meaning in a strengthened resolve to render his brethren service with the same fidelity and devotion which he expects from them in his own hour of need.

Moses' Rod

Emblem of Authority

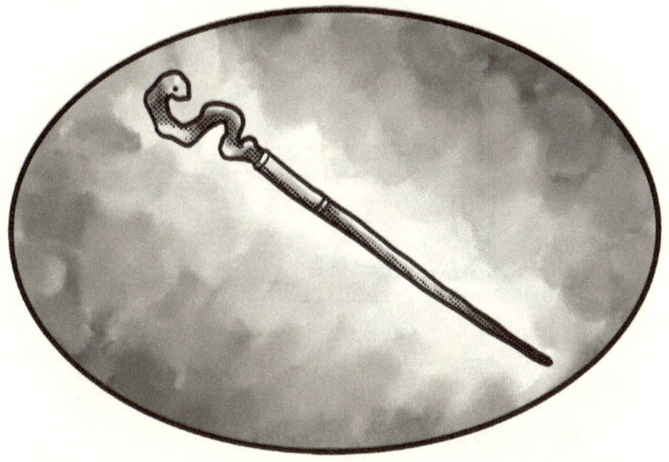

This emblem represents the Rod used in the wonders which God wrought by the agency of Moses for the deliverance of his people, and thus reminds us of that great Lawgiver. In the idea of authority are included those of discipline, correction and support, for God's rod is spoken of as a soother and sustainer – "Thy rod and Thy staff they comfort me," said the Psalmist. Probably the long rod or staff used in traversing mountainous paths was meant. Thus the Odd Fellow is taught to be such a comforting and sustaining Rod to the weak, the needy and the afflicted.

Noah's Ark

Emblem of Preservation

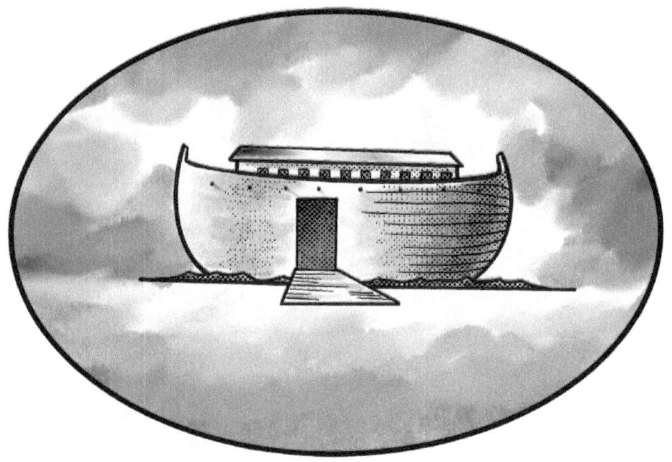

This emblem represents the divinely appointed means for saving the few who repeopled the world; it teaches us "to give heed to every divine admonition, and seek every refuge of grace provided for us." It reminds us that we should make use of every lawful means to preserve a brother, or one under our protection. We are preserved that we may bless others, and commanded to bless, that we may be blessed.

The Horn of Plenty

Emblem of Abundance

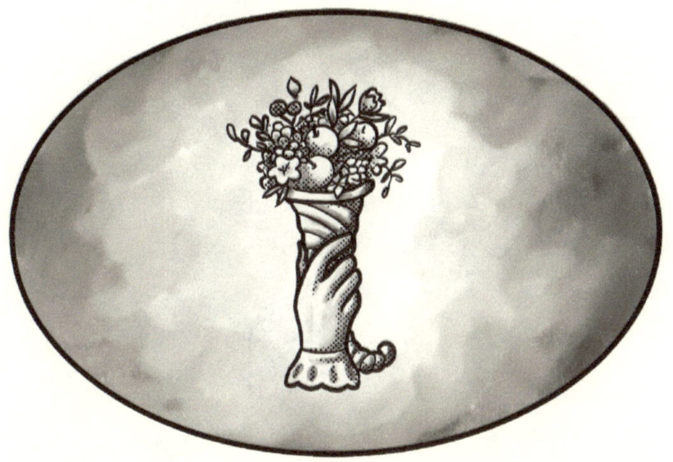

This is the representation of a memory stored with knowledge, wisdom, and goodness by the exercise of industry in acquiring and wise frugality in treasuring up for use. It reminds us that the end of acquisition is, that we may abound unto others and find increase in giving. It teaches us to gather knowledge and wisdom, especially that Divine Wisdom which, rising above the merely selfish and clannish, shall teach us to behold man and his true interests in the light from above. It also includes in its instruction the lesson that if we are faithful in the discharge of our duty, we shall ever find in the resources of our Order an ample supply for our wants.

The Dove

Emblem of Peace

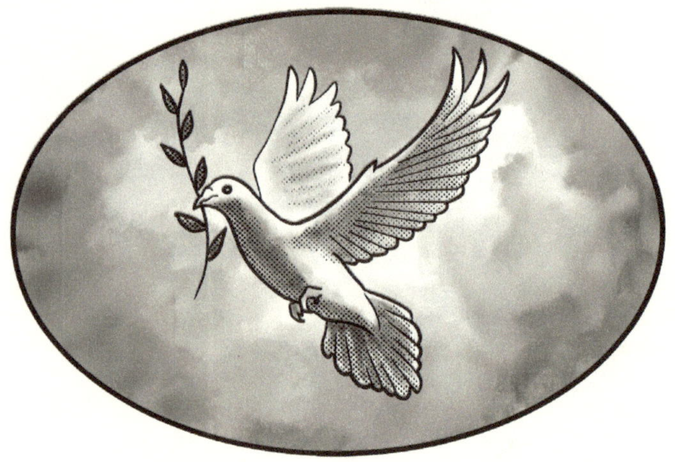

The messenger of peace and goodwill, of promise and of hope – what lot more happy and more desirable than thine! "Like a tree planted by the rivers that bringeth forth his fruit in season, thy leaf shall not wither, and whatsoever thou doest shall prosper." Be not weary in thy progress. Go forth ever in the cause of friendship – bear ever the olive-branch of peace to the oppressed.

Aaron's Budded Rod

Emblem of Instruction

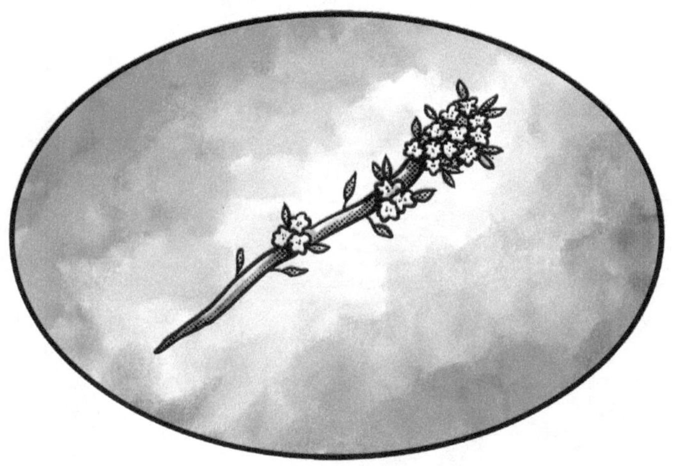

This emblem reminds us of Aaron, who ministered at the holy altar and spoke the words of divine life to the people. By this emblem the Odd Fellow is taught that he, himself, should represent the owner of that rod. To "speak the Truth in Love" is a cardinal duty of our Order. It is your office, your right and your duty to correct the errors and confirm the trust of your brethren, and to illustrate the principles of Friendship and Love with all the power of Truth. And as divine truth from Aaron's lips gave life to the dried wood, so it will give interest, knowledge, life to the lessons of our rituals and emblems, if you will but speak it in the demonstration of its Spirit and its power.

The Beehive

Emblem of Industry

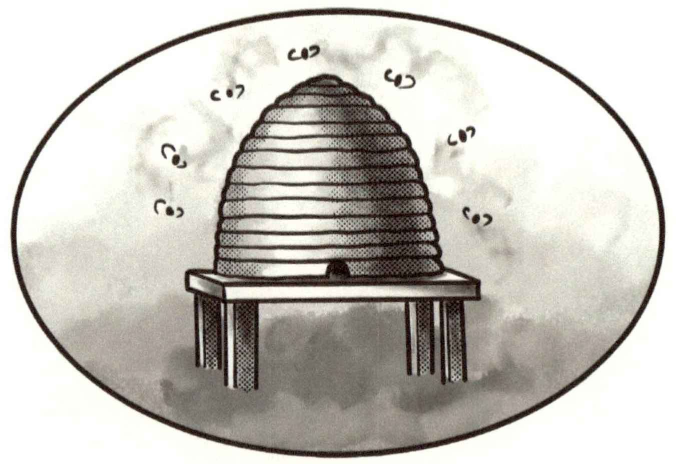

This emblem represents order and unity in working, and reminds us of our obligations to meet together as one family, to aid and relieve those in distress. It likewise teaches us the distribution of tasks and labors to accomplish common aims, and urges us to shun idleness, and all misuse of time and of means. No man can be happy unemployed. No matter how rich he may be, he must work if he would not be miserable. As members of this order, we must labor – if not for ourselves, then for our fellows.

The Shepherd's Crook

Emblem of Guidance

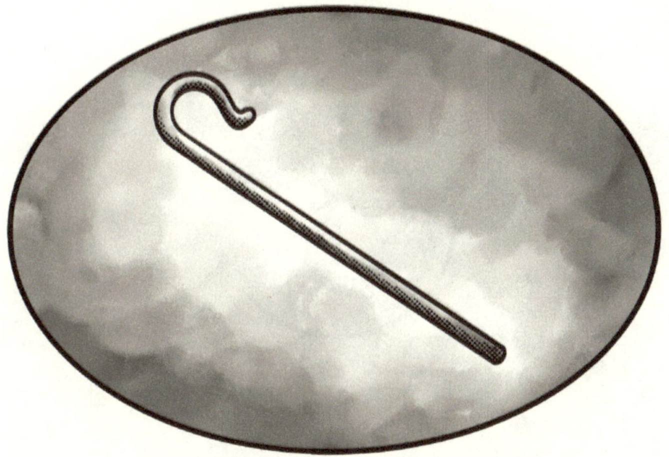

This emblem represents the implement whereby the shepherd directs his flock in its migrations, and protects his sheep from the wolves; and it reminds us of those others who have led and defended us so that we, in turn, might be good shepherds to. all those placed under our care and influence.

The Globe in Clouds

Emblem of the World of Mankind

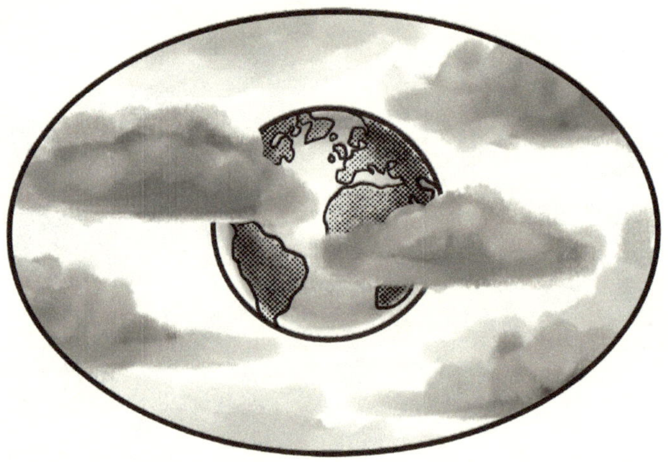

The globe in clouds represents the earthly home of man, the field of our life-efforts and labors, the nursery of immortality. It reminds us that the world in which we have now advanced, and put forth our hand anew for greeting and labor, is still partly in clouds; and teaches us that as light is dispersing those clouds, so may our light aid in dissipating the ignorance which yet obscures those true relations that bind man to his Creator and his fellow-man. It thus incites us to meet together as brethren, and apply the light and warmth augmented and strengthened by our union wherever ignorance needs the one, or want and woe the other.

The Globe in Sunlight

Emblem of the Regenerated World

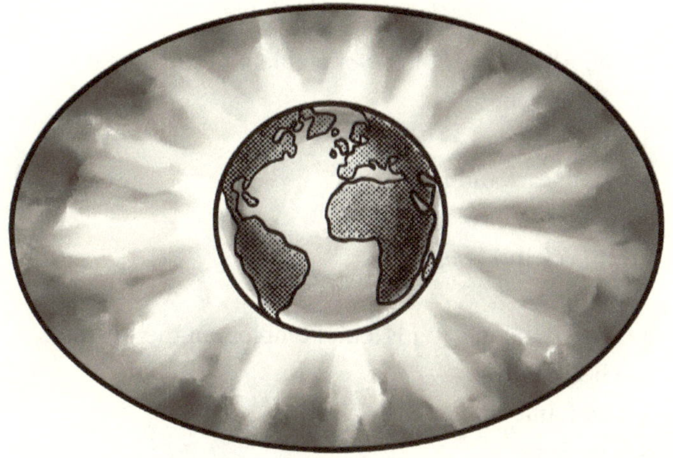

The globe in sunlight represents "the world, and they, that dwell therein" as beheld in its Creator's purpose when "God saw everything He had made, and behold, it was very good" – as seen by the heavenly hosts in visioned future, "when the morning stars sang together. and all the sons of God shouted for joy" – and as it will be seen in reality, when purified by the sanctifying influences of Friendship, Love, and Truth, and of Faith, Hope and Charity. By contrast with the globe in clouds, it reminds us of the world as it is, of the world as it should be, and of our solemn duty to "go on" through all temptation and trial to virtue and victory at last.

Rev. A.B. Grosh's "Odd Fellow's Improved Manual" of 1876 lists the relationship between the full set of 32 emblems then in use, and the nine degrees of the Order, as these latter existed before the revisions of the 1880s that created our current degree sequence. The list runs as follows:

Initiatory Degree

1. The All-Seeing Eye (chief emblem of the degree)
2. The Three Links
3. The Axe
4. The Heart and Hand

First (White) Degree

5. The Globe in Clouds (chief emblem of the degree)
6. The Beehive
7. The Lamb
8. The Sun

The Second (Covenant or Pink) Degree

9. The Bundle of Sticks (chief emblem of the degree)
10. The Quiver and the Bow
11. The Three Arrows
12. The Rainbow
13. The Stone Ezel

The Third (Royal Blue) Degree

14. Moses' Rod (chief emblem of the degree)
15. Noah's Ark
16. The Dove

17. The Serpent

The Fourth (Remembrance or Green) Degree

18. Horn of Plenty (chief emblem of the degree)
19. The Scales
20. The Sword

The Fifth (Scarlet) Degree, or Priestly Order

21. Aaron's Rod (chief emblem of the degree)
22. The Coffin
23. The Moon and Seven Stars
24. The Bible

The Patriarchal Degree

25. The Tent (chief emblem of the degree)
26. The Shepherd's Crook
27. The Three Pillars

The Golden Rule Degree

28. The Altar of Incense (chief emblem of the degree)
29. The Tables of the Law

The Royal Purple Degree

30. The Ark of the Covenant (chief emblem of the degree)
31. The Hourglass and Scythe
32. The Globe in Sunlight

Sources

Anonymous, "Revised Odd Fellowship Illustrated" (Chicago: Ezra Cook & Co., 1911)

Beharrell, T.G., Rev., "Odd Fellows Monitor and Guide" (Indianapolis: Robert Douglass, 1890).

Donaldson, Paschal, "The Odd Fellows' Pocket Companion" (Cincinnati: R. W. Carroll & Co., 1875).

Grosh, Rev. A. B., "Odd Fellows Improved Manual" (n.1.: n.p., 1876).

Ridgely, James. L., "History of American. Odd Fellowship" (Baltimore: By the author, 1878).

Ross, Theodore, "The Illustrated History of Odd Fellowship" (NY: Ross History Co., 1916).

9 781962 533003